TO:

Enjoy

Blue Collar Poetry

of the Mind, the Heart, and the Soul

Sincerely

Hugh McHugh

Hugh McHugh

American Literary Press, Inc.
Baltimore, Maryland

Blue Collar Poetry
of the Mind, the Heart, and the Soul

Library of Congress
Cataloging in Publication Data
ISBN 1-56167-205-X

Published by

American Literary Press, Inc.
8019 Belair Road, Suite 10
Baltimore, Maryland 21236

Manufactured in the United States of America

Acknowledgments

Nobody writes alone. To all the people in my life who have given of themselves and especially to my wife Maura who has tolerated all my ups and downs while writing these poems. I dedicate these poems to Maura, Jack and Mary Ann Dudley, and Barbara and J. J. Quinn for all their help and support.

To all the people in my life,
And especially my pretty wife,
To Jack Dudley and his wife Mary Ann,
For their computer help and plotting out a plan.
And most of all my special Polish chick,
She married Quinn and with her mind so quick,
She kept me straight with comments and wit,
And helped me appreciate a little English Lit.
But most of all I thank my God
For all His help and a good prod,
No words would be written on any page,
And the world would be without another sage.
These simple words are for any man,
And were written in modesty without a plan.
To be enjoyed by one and all,
In the winter, summer, and the fall.

November 9, 1994

This book is dedicated to my Mother and Father in Ireland.

Table of Contents

Poems of the Mind

Poems of the Heart

Poems of the Soul

Poems of the

Mind

A Fallen Leaf

It's that time of year to watch the leaves fall,
From trees so graceful, tall, and small.
The leaves hang limp, resigned to their fate,
Their color changing to yellow and gold of late.
A leaf sailed off a limb so high,
It bounced among the branches still so spry,
Sailing one way then changing course,
It headed towards the earth and it's source.
It landed softly on the ground with a sigh,
Looking at it's home in the tree so high,
Where it used to be so proud and free,
Casting it's head around in that tree,
So proud above the earth's brown soil,
So strong and green and free of toil.
Alas, the north wind came with a cry,
Saying, "It's time for you to fall and die."
It choked off all the food and sap,
And then it sprang it's frosty trap,
'Til the leaf could no longer hold onto life,
So, it fell to the ground, an end to its strife.
Cast around by the wind with a mournful sound,
To rot, to change, to be eaten or ground,
To change from yellow to brown and black,
To be raked up, picked up, or put in a sack.
It lies there wondering what its fate will be,
No longer a part of the big high tree.
And so the leaf bids farewell to the world,
As its life fades away and it becomes mould,
To feed again that bare high tree.
When Spring melts Winter and sets life free.

9/28/93

Art

Art is the blossoming of the imagination.
It's painting a picture and not stagnation.
It's using your hands to frame out the picture.
It's using your eyes to color the fixture.
It's mixing the colors and blending them, too.
It's sketching the landscape and painting the sky blue.
It's catching the shadows of clouds passing by,
As they change all the colors and darken the sky.
It's the stopping of time and the people within,
It's bringing alive the flesh and the skin.
It's catching the look in the eye of a woman.
The smile on her face that makes her so human.
The leaves on the trees as they shake and billow.
The child on the swing as she sits on the pillow.
The never ending color of flowers in the garden.
The bow of the waiter as he begs her pardon.
The style of the clothes or the mix and match.
The checks, or the tweeds, or even the patch.
The shoes that reflect the time and age.
The hair style of the waiter and the page.
The position of the sun tells the light what to do,
As it reflects through the trees and on the water so blue.
And when it's all finished, we hope it looks right,
A picture that warms us with color and light.

5/16/94

4

Dancing

I remember the first time I went to a dance.
I did not know whether to walk or to prance.
All the girls congregated on one side of the floor.
All the men on the other side not far from the door.
How do we cross that space that lies in between us,
And ask her to dance without making a fuss?
It baffles my mind how to ask for a dance.
So I rehearse it many times and now is my chance.
The music strikes up and I summon up my courage,
To go ask a girl in that large entourage,
And when she says, "yes," my mind goes blank,
For now it is time to dance and my heart just sank,
For my feet feel so awkward and so clumsy and big,
It's difficult to get them to move to the music of a jig.
I stepped on her toes and I kicked her on the shin,
It's the first time I'm dancing and the only way to begin.
I left a lasting impression on that girl's mind.
If I ask her to dance again she will act as if blind.
But the music soon flows from the mind to the feet,
And I start to get better and also learn the beat.
And now I can dance all day and all night,
And move around the floor like a bird in flight.
So thanks to those brave women who took all those blows,
When I first started my dancing and prancing on their toes.

3/5/94

Don't Judge

I don't judge people by their color or creed,
Nor by their wealth or poverty, or if in need.
I don't look at my friends and judge them today,
As I go off to church and to my God pray.
Because all of my judgements are liable to be wrong,
So I must accept them as they are, and learn to be strong,
In faith and in the belief that Jesus was right,
When He saved Mary Magdalene from her terrible plight.
Let him who is without sin cast the first stone.
Yes, I know I have wronged and I must atone,
For the way I have treated people, day after day,
My friends and relatives, and sometimes think it's play.
It's not what goes into my mouth that will really count,
But what comes out daily that will balance the account.
Now it's time for a man like me to look back and say,
"Father forgive me my sins that I commit each day."
My judgements are clouded, and to God I must pray,
To keep me on the right path because I'm made of clay.

3/5/94

Dreams

Dreams come fleetingly in the middle of the night
They are in perfect vision and sometimes give me a fright.
I struggle with them, because they are so real.
My mind doesn't realize it, and they become a big deal.
They are sometimes very pleasant, and I want them back,
But no matter how hard I try, I just wake up in the sack.
They can be so beautiful and an answer to a prayer,
So I enjoy them and hold them as long as I dare.
And when I awaken, I feel so alone and sad,
I've lost all the good feelings, and that's too bad.
When I am dreaming and running away from my fears,
And wishing I could wake up because I'm hurt and in tears.
The tension makes me wake up and draw a deep breath,
And I thank God I am awake and not facing death.
Sometimes when I have been dreaming all through the night,
I can't seem to remember them and I get all uptight.
Good sleep and good dreams are rare and a real find,
But that's not the way it usually happens in the mind.

3/7/94

Drink Up, It's Good for You

I drink at the bar on the corner of Main Street.
It's an old place, you know, and not very neat.
All the locals go there to drink and to share,
And I spend my hard-earned money without a care.
It's dark and secluded with smoke-filled air.
The smell of beer and booze is everywhere.
The bar stools are filled with people who swear;
They sit and they drink and they pass some air.
The conversation always seems to be the same,
About money and the races and playing the game.
It's a wonder how I spend so much of my time,
Sitting sipping or drinking my beer or vodka and lime.
Sometimes the bartender changes once, or maybe twice,
They talk about each other and it's not nice.
The booze takes its toll on my body and my brain,
It loosens my tongue and brings on some pain.
I eat no food and I continue to drink,
My senses are dulled and I begin to blink.
My muscles are loose and my talk begins to slur.
And it isn't too long before things begin to blur.
I stagger out into the cold night air,
Trying to find my way home and I'm in despair.
I hang onto things and then fall on my face,
And nobody wants to know me because I'm a disgrace.
And somehow I struggle and manage to get home.
I then bang on the door or call on the phone.
I wake up the children, and all the neighbors hear,
As I holler and curse and play on their fear.
And through all this racket I could hear my wife hiss,
Why am I acting like an animal and has life come to this.
I say I only go out drinking because it's the company I miss.
But all I find is trouble, and I wind up going amiss.
Bad luck to the drink as my mother used to say,
Because there's so many better ways to spend my pay.

1/1/94

Flying

Man watched the eagle as he soared in the sky,
And said, "How great it would be if I could fly."
He tried using wings and they were a big flop.
He now added motors, and many ended with a cough.
Then one day in North Carolina after many, many trials,
The Wright brothers lifted off the ground with big smiles.
That started the tide of men flying in the air,
And people from all places came to watch and to stare.
The machines grew bigger and faster with time,
And now are used for everything, to include war and crime.
They called them airplanes and they started airlines.
They flew faster and faster; it was a sign of the times.
We'll break the sound barrier and we'll travel in space,
And we'll do it in machines of beauty and grace.
We went from the piston to the jet engine in time,
And then, lo and behold, in nineteen fifty-nine,
We shot into outer space and started a new race
To the Moon, and the stars, and to any other place.
Our first goal was the Moon, and we said it would be soon,
We had to develop a machine to travel on the Moon.
Ten years after this our rockets were big and strong,
So we headed for the Moon and landed Neil Armstrong.
"What a feat," we said, as we counted our dead.
We hardly had started and our economy was bled.
Now we need a new invention that is good and cheap,
To be able to visit the stars for a price not so steep.
We learned the Earth was not flat, but beautiful and round,
And we've come into a new age and are mentally bound,
To investigate outer space with the help of God's grace,
And let's hope, as a people, we can keep up the pace.

2/1/93

Golf

I drive to the course in the countryside.
I take out my bag and walk with a stride,
Into the clubhouse and plunk my bag down,
"We'll do eighteen today," and I see the starter frown.
"There's no openings right now, so you'll have to hold on
Until the other fours have hit and they are all gone."
We stand and we putt and we swing our clubs.
We listen for our names and we show him our stubs.
We are up now to play and we hit the little ball.
I wind up in the trees and hear the birds call.
We search for a while and then I drop one down.
I am on the green in five and I feel like a clown.
The hole seems so small and the ball so big.
So, I hesitate and stop and take a small swig.
We continue to hit and follow the ball.
It doesn't go where it's supposed to at all.
It's lie is never good or I'm in the rough.
I started out so fresh and now it's getting tough.
And when I am finished I sign the card and complain,
About my shoes, my club's and I'm feeling the strain.
So ends the day at the golf club for me.
I've gotten rid of my frustrations on the ball, you see.
I go home to my wife and she truly can see,
What a tough day I've had, as I drink my ice tea.

1/14/94

Great Intentions

The world is full of great intentions,
But in the end they get no mentions.
They are made of air and part of talk,
But never get up or learn to walk.
"I will do this, and I will do that,"
And then the kid turns out to be a brat.
"I'm not supposed to get my hands dirty,"
And walks around saying life is so murky.
Great intentions are made while sitting down,
And unless we get up the intentions drown.
For doing and saying are two different things,
One stands still and the other swings.
Great intentions always remain on the seat.
And the longer they wait, the greater the defeat.

3/8/94

Honesty

Honesty, they say, is the best policy.
It keeps the mind in line and throws out fallacy.
It's the basic ingredient in my life today,
And no matter what happens I know it must always stay.
For dishonesty is something that makes people glare,
It has the tendency to return and leave my soul bare.
The legacy of honesty gives richness to my life,
And when I tell the truth I have no worry or strife.
For honesty and wisdom go hand in hand.
Dishonesty and lies disappear like sand,
They sift through the fingers and leave the hand bare.
And your friends walk away and leave you standing there.
Honesty pays off and is not a crime.
It leads to great riches time after time.
Dishonesty is like building a castle in the air,
It's built on lies and is full of despair.
Now honesty starts off on a good foundation,
And God is always pleased with this new creation

3/10/94

Hunting

I took the gun and put it under my arm.
It's been there a lifetime and never caused any harm.
The two old shotguns and the twenty-two
Stood in the corner with the cartridge belt, too.
And none of the children put a hand on them.
They were used to go hunting for fowl in the glen.
Shot grouse, or partridge, or the fox that killed the hen.
Woodcock, wild duck, or the turkey that escaped the pen.
We thinned out the deer so that they could live and eat,
And we filled up our freezers with venison meat.
Shot the goose and the pheasant with his feathers so grand,
We cleared off the rabbits from the farmer's land.
The owners greeted us warmly because we balanced the books,
Or otherwise there would be no wheat to make the stooks.
We eat like kings and we grew strong and tall,
And we also have some trophies to hang on the wall.
Our guns were used for hunting and the good of the land,
And were never used for evil or by a robbers hand.

1/22/94

Imagination

Imagination to me is the creativity of my mind.
It's something I'd have even if I were blind.
It's a gift from God because I care.
To open up my mind and to lay it bare.
To see things so different, so vibrant and new,
While arranging them and sorting them just like a crew.
It's a real gift to me and those who persevere,
As we look for the answers where none appear.
It's seeing things now that don't exist,
Or taking things that are, and giving them a new twist.
It's watching the birds and learning to fly,
It's going to the moon on our very first try.
It's sailing the oceans just as we please,
And going under it and over it with the greatest of ease.
It's travelling to places where we've never been before,
While inventing new engines with power galore.
It's going out into space and opening the door,
It's travelling through the body as never before.
It's seeing God's creations and wondering if there's more.
It's tackling all our problems and trying to feed the poor.
My imagination is only limited by laziness and sloth,
And sometimes negative attitudes, or ignorance, or both.

3/12/94

Life

Life has its ups and its downs.
Its threadbare clothes and its gowns.
Its arguments and making up.
Its shining moments and in the cups
It's marriage and children and a lot of work.
It's sweat and tears and sometimes pork.
It's making up and saying I'm sorry.
It's holding your tongue and a lot of worry.
It's birth and death, and joy and sorrow.
And there are times when we must borrow.
It's kindness, tenderness, anger, and love.
It's seeking help from God above.
It's time and tide and getting old.
It's fire and water, heat and cold.
It's wisdom and understanding and picking a good wife.
It's fortitude and knowledge and living a good life.
It's rearing the children and washing their hands.
It's growing old and grey so gracefully and grand.
It's sickness and health and eating the right food.
It's controlling my temper and staying in a good mood.
It's cooking and cleaning, and sex and fun.
It's wishes and dishes, the mop and some sun.
It's sadness and joy all rolled into one.
It's been that way since time begun.
It's all of these and then some more.
For God made sure life would not be a bore.

8/26/94

Life Today

I dwelt upon my life today,
And I am sad and sorry to say,
That I placed emphasis on the wrong things,
As I tied myself up with worldly strings.
My eyes and my mind were fastened to a spot,
On money, success, possessions, and the lot.
I had them all and I still feel empty,
And now my life is humpty dumpty.
"Where do I go from here," I say,
I'm no longer young and my hair is grey.
My heart is weary and my mind is slow,
For I no longer have youth or its glow.
My time is coming to an end, I know.
I shrink and I blink as I watch the snow.
The cold brings shivers that sink to the bone,
As I sit by the fire and eat a scone.
I'm afraid of the dark and afraid of the night,
And I watch every penny and hold on tight.
For I fear that age doesn't bring me peace and grace,
Only wrinkles and spots and an ugly face.
My knowledge and youth are no longer there,
As I watch how the old are not treated with care.
They sit in old homes and stare into space,
And are calling on the Lord to die in his grace.
What an end to a life that should be full of delight,
When instead we are dying from fear and from fright.

12/1/93

Money

Money, they say, is the root of all evil.
It's another tale spun by the boll weevil.
It is paper with pictures of people on it.
A promise to pay hopefully, a little bit.
We use it to buy just about everything,
But its value keeps falling and depreciating.
They print it in Washington on fourteenth street.
You can hardly hear yourself as the machines repeat,
As they pump out the paper to keep up with the beat,
So, the mounds pile up, and they call it a great feat.
The time will come when we'll have to stop the whole lot,
Because there won't be any more gold or silver in the pot.
They've forgotten the tune and now follow the beat.
They've sold all our butter, our bread, and our wheat.
Now they stand in the Capitol and act as if wise.
They act like they are God and are in for a surprise.
For the time is coming when we'll have to pay,
For all the false paper we've printed day after day.
Starvation and pestilence is what they've bought,
While thinking they are mighty and always sought.
The day of reckoning is coming fast,
And we'll be left standing like dust in the past.
They'll whoop and they'll cry and say it's not fair,
But the money will be all gone and the cupboard bare.
They will stand in awe at how we went bust,
They've forgotten, you see, that it's in God we trust.

1/15/94

Observation

I learn how to live from observing life.
I see what I want to see without any strife.
I look at the wind and adjust my sails,
By using the keenness of my mind so my heart prevails.
I interpret life from the vision of my eyes.
I hope they are seeing right and there are no lies.
It's noting and recording the good things in life.
It's enjoying life fully and picking a good wife.
It's choosing the right course and making the right choice.
It's discarding the bad things and living without vice.
It's watching attentively and developing my mind.
It's being honest and sincere and trying to be kind.
It's seeing the goodness in man and discarding the bad.
Which nearly always guarantees me that I won't be sad.
Observing and following is accepting life as seen.
And hopefully my vision is not always green.
This information is fed to my heart and my mind,
And I pray they sort it out and not as if blind.

7/28/94

Raindrops

Out of the sky they come, saturating my body as they fall.
They bounce off the pavements and drench the trees so tall.
They come by the millions and they call them raindrops.
And when it rains, it pours, and then it stops.
They wash the earth and refresh the grass and trees.
They fill up the rivers that flow down to the seas.
They cool the earth down and turn the grass green.
They are the essence of life and by that I mean,
All life would cease without them, you see,
Because it's a commodity used daily by you and by me,
For washing and cleansing and keeping thirst at bay.
They wet the earth down, and quench fires day after day.
Without them the earth would turn into rock and sand,
All plants would wither away, an end to farmland.
There would be no clouds and the seasons would disappear,
And the sun would burn us up, as we waited in fear.
For without God's hand and His sprinkles from above,
We would disappear off the earth, like taking off a glove.

5/25/94

Rivers

Most rivers start off with a few little wells.
Water following elevations of the valleys and dells.
It eats at the land, and forms its own bed.
It starts as a stream and picks up the watershed.
The rain comes down and the streams overflow,
We now call them rivers as they begin to grow.
They pick up the salt, the minerals, and the lime,
They carry them down and deposit them in time.
Now rivers come in all sizes, some big and some small.
Some are long, some are short, and some have a waterfall.
Some are narrow, some are wide and may have a lake besides.
Some are deep, some are shallow, and some even have tides.
Some have fish, some have fowl that come and go
With the changing of the weather and sometimes the flow.
Some have flowers and reeds so beautiful and grand,
And the animals drink daily and live in them and on land.
Some rivers run swiftly, and some meander on down,
Through the valleys and woods and cities and towns.
Man travels on them daily with boats of every kind.
We fish, and we ski, and sail using the wind.
We build great dams and create reservoirs so grand,
That cover vast areas of grass, trees, and land.
And from these great watersheds, we drink, wash, and clean.
And we power up our motors to service our houses unseen.
Rivers turn the great turbines that turn night into day,
And give us electricity to use in every way.
Rivers feed the lakes with fresh water so we can play,
And let the fish spawn in their sand, when ready to lay.
They keep all human nature refreshed and satisfied,
And so we thank God each day for keeping us supplied,
With the rain and the snow that travels through the sand,
To create the rivers, or we would disappear off the land.

2/7/94

School

School was instituted with a purpose in mind:
To give knowledge to those who see and are blind,
To raise our consciousness, to instruct and train,
To test our skill and put knowledge in the brain,
To develop us mentally and morally for life,
To teach us how to be gregarious, and how to handle strife,
To guide us in our studies and in the arts of every kind,
To increase our knowledge of the world and also mankind.
There is so much to learn in this complex world today,
That we only learn a little no matter how long we stay.
A little knowledge, however, is a dangerous thing,
So lets stay in school and try to learn everything.
Now that's nigh impossible, because it would take too long.
We don't have the time, and it would also be wrong,
For work must take precedence at some time in our life,
Particularly if we get married and have a family and wife.

2/6/94

Shopping

Going shopping is what few men like to do,
But it's something women seem to look forward to.
They like to go shopping and finding a sale,
Saying, "I saved you so much money," and I go pale.
"It only cost two hundred and that was half price,"
As she showed me one dress that looked very nice.
And wait until you see what I got for you,
While she hides all the other packages, oh so new.
The credit cards look shiny from all the use today,
And she is smiling and happy like a child at play.
"The Spring sale will be next week," is all I hear,
As she sits and talks with her friend over a beer.
We'll get there early before all the others,
And buy for the children just like good mothers.
We'll hurry home and have them try them out,
And return them quickly if they don't fit, no doubt.
"I'm sure my husband will scream," I hear her say,
But that's to be expected, it's the American way.
What else can we do who are home all the time,
But spend all the money right down to the last dime.
For shopping is what makes our country so great,
And for the husbands to work hard to pay the freight.

1/26/94

Silence

Silence is golden and is difficult to find.
It is peaceful and pleasant and restful for my mind.
It sharpens my senses and is difficult to hold.
It's pleasant to my body, especially now that I'm old.
It's a quality on earth that is rare and disappearing.
I must travel a long way, so I can keep it appearing.
My ears yearn for peace, so rare and such a delight.
I find it in the early morning or just before night.
It's when all is still, and the wind ceases to blow.
When the trees are at rest and the meadows lay low.
I can sense the stillness, the quiet, and the smell.
It seeps right into my body and makes it well.
It's only there for a short time for me to enjoy.
It's that sense of in between that was easy as a boy,
When I could hear my heart and think the world had stopped.
It's such an awareness of life that can't be topped.
It's not like the quiet that creeps across the land,
As the thunder clouds gather in a mighty band.
That deadness and solemnity that presages a great storm,
And tells all the sea birds to come in from the horn.
That silence is ominous and awesome to behold,
As I wait in the stillness for the action to unfold.
The quiet before the storm has a threatening affect,
And is not very soothing to my body or intellect.
I am a lover of quiet and peace, you can see,
It's at times like these, I can pray and feel free.

8/26/94

Success

Success is something we all seek and desire.
It can be very simple or a great empire.
It's as fleeting today, as the mist in the morn,
And even when we achieve it, it can be a big thorn.
Success brings responsibility, and an image to uphold.
It's only for the aggressive, the brave and the bold.
We strive day and night and when it's in our grasp,
We are so tired and weary, we give out a gasp.
Success is something I create in my mind,
It can be money or love and is sometimes color blind.
We chase after it daily and then you'll have to agree,
That when we catch up to it, it's not what we want to see.
For success is only getting what I've already got,
And when it's in my hands, it is sometimes too hot.
My mind has changed many times over the years,
And I'm tired of chasing success and also the fears.
For success for me, now, is saving my soul.
It's quite a challenge and also my last goal.
Trying to live each day as if it is my last,
Because I don't know when the die will be cast.

3/11/94

Television

I remember when it first came to our town.
It was a small fuzzy picture of a circus clown.
They put it in the window for show and for style.
It was something like the movies, and it made us smile.
They said one day it will be in everybody's house.
Few of us believed them, as we watched the little mouse.
We said, "It was only a novelty, this simple device."
It grew on us daily and now we are paying the price.
It's now at the point where we call it the "Boob Tube."
As we sit and we watch and wonder who is the boob.
It used to bring shows of values and love,
But now it's just mayhem, murder, push, and shove.
We also use it now as a baby sitting machine,
And that's why our children are so nasty and mean.
They do what they see on the television each day.
It's nothing to kill, just like sticking a bale of hay.
No wonder our crime rate is soaring to the sky,
As we watch the list grow daily of those who die.
And the question they ask is, "Why did you do it today?"
"Because I felt like it," is what they generally say.
Why should we convict them when their heroes today,
Kill their enemies on TV as if it is child's play.
The sad thing about it is, it seems to be alright,
To kill without reason because they think they are right.
Now it's time to evaluate the damage done to date,
To our children's young minds, before it's too late.
Nobody seems to care and the violence grows worse,
As the television owners think only of the purse.
The shows are getting filthier and twisted each day,
As they play with our morals and we watch them decay.
The price is getting steeper and we'll soon have to pay,
For our negligence and indifference in a terrible way.

1/25/94

25

The Clock

The clock is an instrument of time they say.
It keeps me running daily and even while at play.
It never stops for anyone not even the dead,
Or when I am sleeping at night in my bed.
Clocks come in all sizes, all colors and shapes.
They hang on walls, on towers and even now, are on tapes.
They have big hands and small hands and second hands, too.
They ring, and they sing, and they play music for you.
I wonder why it was invented and then called time,
When it doesn't seem to matter or keep us from dying.
We grow older each day, whether there is time or not.
It's preordained by God and that is our lot.
The time when I die is not measured by a clock.
God holds us in His hands, while it goes, tick-tock.
And why did they break it down to twenty-four hours?
Because it gives us some control as if we had powers,
Over life and death and just about everything we do.
That is where we are mistaken because it's limited, too,
Because the measure of time is what we all do,
On this earth as people, and not after we pass through.
It's then we meet our Maker and time is no more,
And hopefully we've done the right things, heretofore.

2/5/94

The Dentist

Going to the dentist is like being shot.
The thought of it always hurts me a lot.
Because when I was young, I had teeth pulled on top,
While he was doing it, I thought my head would pop off,
In those days they didn't know what anesthesia was about.
They never drilled or filled, they just yanked it out.
Today it is different, but the mind can't forget
Those days of torture and the pain we would get.
Now I sit in a chair in the modern dentist's office.
They greet me so cordially, And I smile back like a novice.
"He has two more cavities," is what I hear them say.
"The one in the back is very deep," and I begin to pray.
"Open wide and let's see how bad they really are,"
My imagination starts to work and I wonder if they care.
The needle comes out, and it looks as big as a house.
I feel it pierce through my flesh, and I want to shout.
The anesthesia starts to work and my lip thickens up.
I swallow and breathe and want a drink from the cup.
The drill starts to whine, as he works on the tooth.
I smell the burning and feel him touch the root.
The pieces and saliva gather in the side of my jaw,
I wish I could tell him, take out your paw.
But then it is over, before I begin to choke,
And the tooth is so bad they have to put on a yoke.
To fill up the holes with silver, they say,
But they make me just wonder when it's time to pay.
I leave the office with my jaw hanging down.
I had better brush each day or I'll need a full crown.
And now that I'm home and the work is complete,
I thank God today that I still have my own teeth.

2/2/94

The Government

The government is something we like to pick on each day.
It's those rats in Washington, as we point at them and say
"You don't care about us, and it is obvious to see,
Your concern is only for yourselves and not the family."
We send you to Washington to do the right job,
And all you seem to worry about is filling your own gob.
You write out bum checks and you spend all our money,
You raise our taxes with words dripping with honey.
You go to Washington with a few dollars in your pocket,
You leave there rich and famous just like Davy Crockett.
We wonder how that happens on such a meager pay,
That is government directed in such a controlled way.
We send you to the Capitol for a two or six year stay,
And all you seem to do is take more out of our pay.
Then you come back to us when it's time to vote again,
With your hat in your hand, all you women and men.
You promise us everything out of each side of your mouth,
And you say what we want to hear, that is no doubt.
Then when you are elected you vote the other way,
Because you are now in for years and you start to play,
The game of crooked politics and not honesty today.
And we the poor people just suffer and can only say,
"The next time we'll get them right at the gate,
We'll throw the rascals out and put in a new slate."
We wonder why it doesn't seem to make any difference at all
Because money and power contaminates them, and they fall.
You go with such great ideas, and you all walk so tall,
And you wind up in places you shouldn't be at all.
And you learn to spend our money with callousness and gall,
Leaving us holding the bag with our backs to the wall.
Whatever will come of us when our government is this bad?
For it makes us feel alone, sometimes mad, and also sad.
Whatever has happened to the motto, "In God We Trust?"
When all we seem to hear about is money and lust.
May God help us and keep us in the hollow of His Hands,
And protect us from evil and the Washington Brigands.

2/4/94

The Hunt

I hear the sound of the bugle blow,
Across the meadows and down below.
The bay of the hounds as they follow the fox,
Who has been chosen and let out of the box.
They follow his scent as they lope along.
Their yelping and howling is much like a song.
The master on his gelding so big and so strong,
Blows his horn and is followed along by the throng.
The horses and riders dressed in colors so bright,
Follow over the fields with great expectation and delight.
They break into a gallop and the pace starts to increase.
The horses are now sweating with their riders so obese.
They snort and they grunt as they pound out the ground,
While thundering along with such a merciless sound.
They clear fences and water and jump over stone walls.
Approaching them with speed and of course there are falls.
The fox is getting tired and starts looking for a bed.
The hounds are getting closer and he is in dread.
His fate is fast approaching as he stops and cocks his ear,
To listen for the hounds while his heart is full of fear.
The hounds sense the kill and are now making such a din.
While the horses start to gather and the riders just grin.
It is time for the kill and it is cruel and ugly.
The master and the riders stand by and watch so smugly.
The fox has given them a good run, is what they say,
As they head for the big house to change and play.
It's music and dancing, and tall tales of the day,
No mention of the fox, torn apart in the fray.
They forget about the cruelty, with their noses in the air.
And the rest of us stand by and shake our heads in despair.

9/1/94

The Law

The law is no longer what it used to be.
The shysters have made a mockery out of it, you see.
There were only ten commandments on the books long ago,
And they covered every spectrum of life here below.
They were written in stone by the hand of God.
On Mount Sinai where the prophet Moses trod.
We took the law and changed it to suit each case we try.
And if it doesn't suit us, we create a hue and cry.
And now we have so many laws, on and off the books,
One for every condition to satisfy all the snooks.
The judges and the lawyers are bamboozled every day,
As they try to find justice and get sidetracked on the way.
The case load just builds up as the lawyers delay and delay
While they cry out for more judges and ask for more pay.
God's laws are very simple and we've complicated them all.
With our wigs and our gowns and attitudes in this hall.
For justice has changed and it is visible to all,
That if we continue, we are destined to fall.
Somewhere along the way we've forgotten what is just,
So tangled are we with money, power and lust.
We drag or country down and now we are going bust,
Because we depend on man and not "In God We Trust."

6/18/94

The Moon

I walked outside the other night.
What a pleasant surprise, it was like daylight.
The moon was full and high in the sky,
And the clouds were gone or had passed by.
The moon changed the night and made it silver and bright,
So that all the stars disappeared and were out of sight.
The grass and the trees glistened and were a delight.
As the moon hung its mantle of frost on tight.
It smiled and winked like the man in the moon,
As much as to say, "Are you coming back soon?"
We tried it for years and everything went wrong,
Until we landed on the moon with Neil Armstrong.
He got out and prayed and jumped about,
Then got back in and was away with a shout.
We spent so many millions to see what was there.
Some said it was cheese and some said it was bare
The moon stands so high and so bright in the sky.
It is beautiful and colorful and looks as if shy.
It pulls on the earth and moves the tides.
It travels around us and sometimes hides.
It's such a lovely sight in the middle of the night.
It's a blessing for us and a great savings in light.

1/15/94

The Postman

I see him coming down the street,
Happy and bouncing on his feet.
He brings the mail to every house.
He is timid and quiet like a mouse.
He opens the boxes and puts the mail in,
And closes the lid with a quiet din.
I watch as he moves from house to house,
With parcels and letters without a grouse.
He smiles as his load grows lighter with time,
When his day is done he's earned another dime.
He bring's good news, bad news, the checks and the bills.
Moving steadily through neighborhoods, up and down hills.
And the people only see him a few times a year,
And sometimes even forget to bid him good cheer.
For he is always there and seldom will fail,
To take care of his people in rain snow and hail.
So thank to the man who brings so many joys,
As if he were Santa bringing us daily toys.

12/4/94

The Rabbit

I sat down one day under a tree.
I had walked a long way and was tired, you see.
My eyes closed for a minute in the heat of the sun.
I had nothing for my day but a loaded gun.
I opened up my eyes and there very clear,
Was a large bunny rabbit, scratching his ear.
He hopped about and grazed on the grass.
He wiped his face and he scratched his ass.
He looked at me, watched me, and passed me by.
He didn't know how very soon he could die.
He lay on the ground like a large ball of hair.
His stomach was moving with each breath of air.
His ears stood out like two sails in the wind.
They twitched and they moved like one of a kind.
He turned and he hopped and came close to me.
His little fat jaws chewed endlessly.
A little white tail was stuck on his rear,
And it moved up and down as he hopped here and there.
He blended so well into the grass and the brush,
He was part of nature, the tree and the bush.
He glanced at me once more, as if to say,
"You don't belong here; you are only a stray."
He hopped and he hopped and into a hole ran.
Now I'm back at the beginning where the story began.

1/9/94

33

The Sea

It stretches out to the west, as far as I can see.
It's so quiet and calm now for such a mighty sea.
The tide comes in and the waves crash over the sand,
And pushes itself up, 'til it's nigh on the land.
Then rushes right out while tearing at my feet,
Taking everything with it and it's a balancing feat.
And when the wind gathers, the swell begins to grow.
The waves begin to crash and are no longer low.
The water turns black, then white with foam.
The sea gulls come to land and make it their home.
As the waves grow higher, the boats disappear.
The rain begins to fall and my heart begins to fear.
It's time to tie up, and get out of this storm,
And go home to my house that is cozy and warm.
The sea is no place to be when it's angry and wild.
It will toss me around as if I was a child.
It will take me, and shake me, and smash me right down.
And if I don't respect it, I may even drown.
For there's nothing as peaceful or powerful as the sea,
So, I am careful to respect it and leave it be.

1/10/94

The Sun

I like to watch the sun rise,
And I often wonder at it's great size.
It climbs out of the earth me thinks,
It's big, and red, and then it shrinks.
I wonder how it gets so hot,
When it's high in the sky and only a dot.
Its heat so gentle in the morning air,
When it climbs in the sky, I then go bare.
It beats down on me and burns my skin,
It turns it red and the sweat begins.
It burns away the sweat of the day,
And leaves rings of salt like the tide in the bay.
I try to hide from its scorching rays,
I spread cream on my face and read what it says.
The sun searches me out as it dances with glee,
While it sucks up the moisture from land and sea.
It moves across the sky so clear and blue,
While the earth shimmers and dances under its hue.
As the evening approaches the sun sinks down,
And the earth cools, and sighs, and turns all brown.
At last, comes the time of rest and ease,
When I sit and drink and enjoy the evening breeze.
The sun seems to wink at me, as it slowly disappears,
And I know it's done a good job on my face and ears.

12/23/93

The Tree

This lovely tree stands great and tall.
It spreads its branches over the mall.
Its trunk is so big and its leaves are so small
It grows when it's told and sheds in the Fall
It obeys mother nature all year long.
It serves the birds and the bees for a song.
Its branches give shade in the Summer so hot,
And lovers sit under it, because it's a lovely spot.
In the Fall, it changes colors and brightens the land.
It's yellow, gold and brown painted by God's hand.
Then the leaves fall down and the branches are bare.
It's that time of year that we should give a care.
The wind flares up and shakes the tree.
It blows the leaves around and kills the bee.
The tree stands there quietly in the cold and rain.
It takes what Winter throws at it and never complains,
When it has snow on its bark and icicles that sear.
It waits out the Winter and welcomes in the New Year.
It awakens again to the warmth of the Spring,
Saying, "I'll serve and love you and enjoy your swing."

1/6/94

Trust

Trust is an essential part of my life on this earth.
It's opening up my mind, my soul, and my heart.
It's loving someone so that I can give freely,
And in return, being accepted by them completely.
It's baring my soul and looking for acceptance.
It's seeking forgiveness with sincere penitence.
It's leaving myself open for the kicks and the blows.
It's living a pure life and one that shows.
It's necessary in every occupation as well as in life,
For without it in business there will always be strife.
Trust is the joyful acceptance between God and man.
I can call on Him daily or whenever I can.
He does wonders for me when I'm in distress.
He raises my heart up and clears up the mess.
Ask anything in My Name, and I will give it to you.
What greater trust than this, if I believe it's true.
The love that exists between me and my wife,
Is born out of trust and has lasted through our life.
It's a gift from God and was chosen carefully,
So that me and my wife can sleep peacefully.

8/27/94

Vacation

My body looks forward to that time of year,
When I can let down my defenses and enjoy a beer.
I like to say good-bye to my shirt and my tie,
And forget about work or give it a good try.
I like to load up the car, as the kids say good-bye,
Then we head for the ocean, and our home in the sky.
We eat when we want, and we walk barefoot in the sand.
We stand and we watch as the sea surges up to the land.
We swim in the sea or just lie in the sun,
We rub on some lotion or maybe go for a run.
And when we are finished we are glad to go home,
For we are in need of a rest away from the foam.
So we pack up again and start on our way.
Summer vacation is over, and so is the play.
It was such a blast, but it went by so fast.
And now I'm sad again because the summer is past.

1/20/94

Winter

Winter comes faithfully at the end of the year.
It brings death and cold, and frost and fear.
The trees stand out so bare and stark,
Winter has picked them clean of everything but the bark.
They stand as if frozen and made of stone,
They some times are brown or white as a bone.
They seem to be afraid to move or to shake,
In case the north wind blows and they will break.
The ice clings to the branches like fingers of glass,
It melts in the sun and falls with a smash.
The snow filters down from a sky so grey,
The flakes flit and dance, they clash, and they spray.
The snow builds up slowly on the branches so high,
And it makes the trees look like a part of the sky.
It's splendor unsurpassed, and to this beautiful sight,
Adds a blanket of snow that covers the earth day and night.
The green grass disappears and is replaced by the snow,
And the winter wind blows the flakes into drifts that grow.
The deeper the snow, the colder it gets;
The wind whistles and whines when the sun finally sets.
The snow muffles the sound of my feet in the air,
As I cover myself up with layer after layer.
My breath spews out like the steam from the kettle,
And disappears so fast before it has a chance to settle.
My ears turn red and then blue if left out.
As I blow on my hands and belt them about.
The winter no doubt is the master, it's clear,
In January and February, and at the end of the year.

12/5/93

39

Work

Work is a word that is full of action.
It's movement or something like compaction.
I need to be useful to make me whole.
It must have meaning and also a goal.
A purpose behind it that makes me strive,
To be a better father, mother, or wife.

It's using my energy to better my life.
Building or mending or keeping people alive.
It occupies my mind, my heart and my soul.
It gives me satisfaction and makes me whole.
And sometimes I am tired and in need of sleep.
I must rest my body or I will end up in a heap.

By the sweat of my brow I shall earn my bread,
And most of us do it until we are dead.
I like being useful, helpful and kind.
I long for some praise, it's the food of the mind.
A slap on the back or a decent pay raise,
Goes a long way towards helping me through each phase.

The devil on the other hand, works on the idle mind.
And he never seems to stop until I'm in a bind.
But God I know will help me if I only ask,
It's such a simple prayer and not a big task.
So why don't I ask Him for help today,
And then let go, and let God have His way?

I work all my life for what I say.
For a house, car or farm, or even big pay.
I raise up my children and educate them well.
This is sometimes difficult and can hurt like hell.
Now what is the purpose of all this work and play?
If I don't know my God and I am buried today.

So work and be happy and have a good time.
Watch out for the traps, and stay away from crime.
Life on earth was intended to be good and whole.
To give me satisfaction, a purpose and a goal.
However, life on this earth is only a short time,
So I must invest in the next life, so it is sublime.

God have mercy on me and help me each day.
Help me sort out my problems and show me the way.
I kneel down in prayer and bare my soul.
I am a humble being that needs to be made whole.
For without You, my God, life on earth would be sad.
Now my life has some meaning and I'm thankful and glad.

8/13/94

Poems of the

Heart

Abortion

The word is repulsive, and so is the act,
Because it's killing a baby, and that's a fact.
The people who want it are doing it out of fear;
And the people who perform it are expensive and dear.
They've lost all hope, and they don't want the child.
The clinics are cashing in, and their hands are soiled.
They tear the child apart, and they don't seem to care.
They toss it in the garbage with their noses in the air.
They are butchered by the millions, each day we are free.
Thirty million Americans murdered since seventy three.
They cry out for help in their pitiable and feeble way,
As they die those horrible deaths today and every day.
God will surely hear them as we kneel down and we pray,
"Please stop this killing of babies in the USA."
This country of our's was born and has shared in God's love.
And blessed by Him so many times from the heavens above.
The time will surely come when God will hear their cry,
And the murderers who don't repent will eventually die.
They will stand before God with His scepter and His crown,
For judgement time has come and they will now bow down.
For the power of God is awesome and now will come to bear,
On those who murdered the babies and didn't seem to care.
Their punishment will fit the crime that is what they say,
And they will suffer forever in the same deadly way.
The money they made from their bloody and heinous crimes,
Will sear their souls forever until the end of time.
It frightens me to think of Gods judgement and wrath,
As he watches us continue on our murderous path.

1/25/94

A Friend

A friend in need is a friend indeed.
And some disappear with the greatest of speed.
Good friends always accept me, no matter where I am.
And I enjoy their company in a bus or a tram.
For a friend is a gift I give myself.
And to have one I know, I must be one myself.
I must be able to forgive and drink the good wine,
And throw out the sour grapes now and anytime.
For love is the ingredient, mixed in with some time,
That makes a good friendship down along the line.
Love helps the heart overcome all the knots and the fears,
Then we develop a good friend amid the joy and the tears.
The hardness of the heart and the frost is melted away,
And hopefully our friendship will catch and always stay.
For life on earth without friends is a very lonely place,
And if we don't have any, life is very hard to face.
Our riches are measured by the number of friends we've had,
So, love one another and always try not to stay mad.

3/10/94

An Exile

Uprooted from my childhood dreams and joys.
I was only seventeen, one of those poor country boys.
Thrown into the mayhem of life in the big city.
Not knowing where I was going and without any pity.
My pockets were empty and I did not have a job.
They laughed at my accent and I felt like a clod.
The fear and frustration sunk into my bone.
Was I going to fail in this place and have to go home?
I tramped through the streets and I found me a job.
At the time it did not matter that it paid only a few bob,
Because times were hard and there were millions out of work.
I now got an apartment and was able to pop a cork.
I regained my confidence and also my strength,
Amid rejections and slurs wherever I went.
My faith in my God kept me going each day,
and as the years went by I got much better pay.
There was no one to fall back on, no mom or dad,
And as time passed by I was no longer a lad.
My heart yearned for my youth and a place called home,
So I found me a wife and started my own.
Many years went by and I went back to my village.
The people had changed and there was no tillage.
My dreams and my childhood had vanished forever.
A new sadness crept over me just like a fever.
I had grown up in this land that knew me no more.
It was like I had never been in this village before.
I knew that this longing and yearning must pass.
I must go back to the city of concrete and glass.
My home is no longer here, but far across the sea,
Where my wife and my children are calling out to me.
I must go back to the land that took care of every need,
For it clothed me and fed me, and housed me indeed.
Now the land that I was born in, is forever in the past,
And the dreams of my childhood are finished at last.

8/28/94

Animals

When God made man he made the animals, too.
There was a great flood and He saved them, two by two.
When the flood was over, Noah let them all out,
And they went in all directions and scattered all about.
They multiplied and multiplied and covered all the earth.
Then man began to kill them, his reason, for fun and mirth.
Now their numbers are getting smaller and many are extinct,
And the proudest of them all is the elephant so big and pink.
They just kill them for their tusks and they leave all the meat,
To rot in the plains while they sell the tusks and some the feet.
It's the ivory they are after and they will kill them if they can.
It doesn't matter what the law say's, they don't give a damn.
The elephant, however, is only one part of the animal family,
That we are destroying daily, so quickly and systematically.
And one day the world will wake up, but it just maybe too late,
To find that all the animals have disappeared, state by state.
While the big ships troll the oceans and catch all the fish,
They kill the little dolphins, and process them if they wish.
The whales so big and beautiful are blown right out of the sea,
By these new powerful harpoons with explosives on its tree.
They don't stand a chance and are now disappearing so fast
That unless we do something soon, they'll be a thing of the past.
The beautiful lions and tiger are now so rare and few,
That in not too many years from now, will also be gone, too.
Because the wild areas they live in are dwindling day by day,
And pretty soon the lions and tigers will have no place to play.
We are cutting down our forests and everything in between,
And are killing the vegetation so that nothing now is green.
We have truly made a mess of things, the animals on land and sea,
That it makes me wonder what's in store for my family and me.

2/9/94

Being Poor

I know what it's like because I've been there.
It's not being without money or a cupboard so bare.
Poor is when my soul is lost and I'm full of despair.
It's feeling so down and out and my heart is without care.
When life has no meaning and I wonder why I'm here,
And everything goes wrong as I drown in my beer.
Being poor in spirit is surely the meanest of all,
It drags me into the dumps and I continue to fall.
There is no light in the tunnel, as I crawl and I grope.
I can't find my way out and I've lost all hope.
I thought we were poor when there was nothing in the house,
Not even a crumb that would feed a little mouse.
And yet we were happy because we were a family,
For we were all in it together and shared it happily.
For poverty, I found, was only hunger of the skin,
And not of the soul which was caused by my sin.
I thank God for my faith and the love of my wife,
They've made my life easy and gotten rid of the strife.

3/12/94

Birds

They are so beautiful as they fly in the sky.
We couldn't improve on them or give it a good try.
They sing, and they dance, and they swim and they walk.
They come in such beautiful colors and sometimes they talk.
And some of them are so small that they are hard to see,
But what a glorious creation, just for you and me.
We watch them play and sing and build their nests in the tree,
And we ask, "Where do they all come from," so colorful and free?
They make us smile and warm our hearts and are part of the family.
But even in spite of their beauty we treat them too carelessly.
We hunt them and shoot them, as they take off in flight.
We wonder at their beauty, but we eat them up at night.
Now the birds in the air, just like the animals on the ground,
Are being killed off so quickly, that soon none will be found.
We shoot them and stuff them for trophies every day,
And, they are also running out of places to hide and stay,
For they live and they feed in the same trees, bush, and grass,
Their fate is about sealed and they are also about to pass,
Into a new age just like the dinosaurs of the past,
Where hopefully we will find them in museums in a cast.
So it's good-bye to all birds, so beautiful and pleasant.
And one day our children will say, "What is a pheasant?"

2/9/94

Breakfast

I like to get up to the smell of good food,
To some bacon and eggs or sausage is just as good.
The aroma of fresh coffee awakens my mind,
It's the work of angels and is pleasant and kind.
To be able to sit down and eat a good breakfast each day,
Is a good beginning and starts the day off the right way.
With a smile on my face and a good taste in my mouth.
It stirs up my insides and helps me hurry about.
It awakens my taste buds and refreshes my mind,
And it helps me think fast as I drive to the grind.
It starts off my day right and strengthens me for work,
And prepares me for every test and even the company jerk.
For the day is so taxing if not started off right,
It helps me to get through the day and not get uptight.
Each day my wife makes breakfast for me and my family,
Is like saying, "I love you," and it will always be.
It's one of the nicest things that happen to me each day,
And it's because she does it freely and in a loving way,
That I really appreciate her in a very special way.
So all you men and women who cook breakfast each day,
Accept our thanks and gratitude and hopefully good pay.

2/3/94

Cancer

I sat there and watched him as he died.
There was nothing I could do, and so I cried.
"There is no hope," is all they would say,
And so I went home and I started to pray.
I remembered him well when he was strong and tall.
He was a giant of a man and great with a ball.
He would stand there and laugh, as I tried to pass.
He would take me right down, and I lay in the grass.
He had great strength, and so much gentleness, too.
He was a little boy inside, and that I knew.
He played with such vigor and joy as he grew,
And everyone liked him and loved him, it's true.
And now he lies here just a shadow of the man,
With his eyes sunken back, his skin black and tan.
I watched him disappear, get smaller and become thin.
There was nothing I could do but bear it with chagrin.
I listened to his pain as he tried to talk to me,
My bowels just crawled up and I could hardly see,
For my heart was breaking at this terrible sight,
As I watched him die slowly and I got all uptight.
Why has he to die and in such terrible pain,
While we all stand around feeling the strain.
Then he looked up at me and he tried to smile.
He tried to talk and then had to stop for a while.
"I'm going to a better place," is what he just said.
"God knows who I am," and then he was dead.

12/22/93

Children

The children are a picture that represents you and me,
Because we've taught them everything since they were three.
They have mirrored our actions and believe all we say.
So what we have today is what we made yesterday.
They stood with eyes so bright and always so trusting,
And yet could get into trouble while you were dusting.
They smiled so easily and started to cry just as fast.
Now so loving and joyful, and again test you to the last.
They are a joy to our souls and they can break our hearts.
They pull at our heart strings and can take us apart.
And as they get bigger and smarter they know how to play,
To the tune of mothers good nature, day after day.
For mothers are big softies, and the children know it well,
When something goes wrong there is collusion not to tell.
The father who is out working is always the last to know,
And doesn't find out what has happened for a month or so.
They get so independent and then they follow their peers,
And get into more trouble and then the fears and tears.
It's a game of life that's played each day in every family,
As the children grow and fall in love and leave eventually.
We sigh and say that we can't wait until the kids are gone,
But that never seems to happen as the grandkids come along.

1/21/94

Compliments

Compliments are few and far between.
People would rather nag than build esteem.
Compliments can be too light or laced with syrup.
Some are said with caution and are used as a stirrup.
Compliments have to be pure and said with honesty and pride.
Or they are worse than a lie and trip us up in our stride.
Compliments should raise up our spirits and also our mind,
In a world that is often more nasty than kind.
They must be well received and not with a puffed up chest.
With no swelling of the head is always the best.
Don't knock them or tear them down when given or received.
Accept them with gratitude and always believed.
They come so rarely now and they bring on a glow.
They are the nicest and the choicest of gifts here below.
They don't cost anything but can really increase our power.
They strengthen us and help us to open up like a flower.
The children in this world are so greatly in need,
Of compliments daily to help them develop like seed.
Three compliments a day should be our purpose and goal,
And our inventory of friends will grow to a shoal.

2/24/94

Christmas

It's that time of year
Of happiness and good cheer.
Our hearts are lightened,
Our minds are brightened,
For the Child of Love,
Has come from above,
To sprinkle the earth with love.

It's a time of buying,
A time of wrapping,
A time of tying,
A time of sighing,
A time of hugging,
A time of crying,
A time to say, "I love you."

It's a time of giving,
A time of living,
A time of saying,
A time of praying,
A time of singing,
A time of ringing,
In the joy of life and a happy new year.

Family

It started with Adam and Eve a very long time ago.
A husband and wife and then they begat some more.
They multiplied and spread to countries far and wide,
And the families began to grow just like a living tide.
Now I look at my children, my wife and beyond I see,
That when it's put in writing they call it a family tree.
I have brothers, and sisters, their husbands and wives.
I have uncles, and aunts, and cousins besides.
I have grandpas and grandmas who are so full of pride,
And who can forget the in-laws, and outlaws who hide.
When I put them all together, I have some kettle of fish.
It's not what I would want, if I had my wish;
But that is what makes horse races, and now I see,
That I can't be selective when it comes to family.
For God was very wise when he put us together,
Saying, "Go, and multiply, and love one another."

1/26/94

Failure

Failure is woven into the fabric of our human nature.
We are just a human being and not a perfect creature.
God doled out His gifts and was very generous to us.
He made us in His likeness and that was also generous.
We failed Him in Eden, by eating the apple on the tree.
We no longer felt clean, and no longer felt free.
We fell a long way, and He had compassion on us.
He sent His only son and let Him die on the cross.
His blood wiped out all our failure and our sin,
And He gave us another chance to live and now begin,
To conquer our failures and now to no longer fall,
Into the depths of sin, where evil makes us crawl.
The little failures in life will always be there,
Nothing ventured, nothing gained and always give a care,
Because it's not how far we fall but how high we bounce back,
For the devil never stops and will always continue to attack.
God gives us His grace, by the bucket and the pail,
And He doesn't judge those who try hard and just fail.
But He does expect a return when we up and we die.
And God help those who received and failed to try.

3/1 1/94

Falling in Love

I watched her walk by, as she went her way.
I looked at her and smiled and bid her good day.
She grew on me daily like a limb on a tree,
And I planned to meet her and ask her to tea.
I went over everything I would say in my mind.
I would be gentle, confident, and very kind.
But, when the time came and I was face to face,
I blushed and I stuttered and had very little grace.
She smiled at me shyly and said, "How do you do?"
My answer was fast and I nearly said, "I love you."
We walked, and we talked, and I started to melt.
My heart was beating so fast that in my mind I felt,
"How could this girl have gotten such a grip on me?"
That I could hardly wait each day to be
With her talking, walking and holding hands.
While her smiles melted away all the macho strands.
I did not know what love was like, you see,
But now I was hog tied like a man to a tree.
And what did I do when I got to her place,
I just smiled and held her and kissed her on the face.
It wasn't very long before I bought her some flowers,
And all my friends said to me you've lost your powers.
Her eyes lit up with joy, and to my surprise.
She took me in her arms, and I was now in a demise.
Now she held onto me as we walked down the street.
We were happy and joyful and easy to greet.
It was obvious to me how we treated each other.
It wouldn't be long before I would meet her mother.
Then the day came and I asked her to marry me,
And she said "yes" and betrothed were we.
Now we are old and married and down by the sea,
And we still love one another and drink our tea.

1/5/94

Fishing

The boat chugs quietly as we weave our way out.
The dawn is breaking and our minds are on trout.
Now the bay opens up and we head for the ocean.
The engines start to roar and we jerk with the motion.
The sea crashes around us, as we move through its bowels.
And the spray splashes on us and we use our towels.
And after an hour of racing to the fishing spot,
We start to reel out our rods and hope they are hot.
The fish strikes hard, and the line snaps tight.
I struggle to reel it in with all my might.
My hands are now tired, and there is sweat on my brow.
It feels like I'm pulling in a fish as big as a cow.
When he comes close I see him flash through the sea,
As I pull him in closer, he really tries to get free.
He is big, long, and strong, and a fisherman's dream.
I reel him in, net him, and we pull him in as a team.
He is thirty eight pounds of pure fighting fish,
He is what I had come for, and filled my every wish.
My day is complete now and I am pleased and satisfied.
Whatever I catch after this is a fish on the side.
I take the fish home and show it with zeal,
Then I cook it and we eat it as our evening meal.

1/25/94

Grandma

Grandma sits down every day and watches TV.
She has an opinion on everything from this, you see.
She dolls herself up and puts on one of her wigs,
And joins in the parties and takes a few swigs,
For she is happy to have lasted over eighty years.
She laughs, and she smiles, and sheds a few tears.
Her body has dissipated but not her sharp mind.
She is friendly and courteous, and always kind.
It's something to see and a pleasure to watch,
How she strives to look young in the coffee klatch.
She always stands up and makes a statement of a kind,
That under this old body there's a fine young mind.
And we are glad to have her as part of our family,
For that is the way life is supposed to be.
And her age is her beauty, and she handles it fine,
As she grows older she gets better, just like a wine.

1/18/94

Happiness

Happiness is living and seeing the joy in life,
Being married to a good woman and loving your wife.
It's seeing things colored red, yellow, white, and blue.
Dancing the night away and telling someone, "I love you."
It disappears fast if you forget and don't seem to care,
So make up your mind you won't let it happen anywhere.
Because happiness is loving what you have today,
And don't let success trip you up or get in the way.
Happiness does not come from having many things.
It comes from the inside and of course it always brings,
Only the good things in life to the husband and wife,
Who have learned to live together without any strife.
For God gives His measure to those who are faithful,
To Him and His commandments and those that are grateful.
He says, "Love one another as I have loved you,"
And we'll find a place in Heaven and happiness, too.

3/8/94

I Lost My Job

I lost my job three months ago.
I'm deep in debt and feeling low.
I look at my wife and children and see,
Looks that are there and not supposed to be,
For they know I'm down and in despair,
About losing my job and knowing, it's not fair.
However, all is not fair in love and war,
But they forgot to add my house and my car.
They all disappeared with a stroke of a pen,
When the man at the top decided at ten,
That fifty percent of the work force must go,
To bring down the overhead because things are slow.
"They are only a number to me," he said,
And forgot about our families in need of bread.
We look forward to a new year with profit up high,
So we can all get a big bonus and not have to cry.
But there's someone above who handles the till,
And when it's time for His graces, He will balance the bill.
Now I raise up my hands like a child in prayer,
Saying, "My God where are You, in this time of despair?"
My resume's are out, and I'm willing and able.
Please help me today to put bread on the table.
And, lo and behold, He answers my prayer.
"You're there, Lord, I know and thanks for Your care."

12/3/93

Ireland, Free At Last

I look down from on high and what do I see,
An island so green in the middle of the sea.
It looks so quiet and peaceful you'd think it was free.
But England and its soldiers say that is not to be.
She sent her armies to Ireland over three hundred years ago.
They were battled to a standstill but didn't want to go.
They signed peaceful agreements with Sarsfield in his glen,
To respect all Irish rights and also its Catholic men.
They broke all their treaties and then proceeded at will,
To slaughter the Irish Catholics until they had their fill.
They issued proclamations against teachers and priests.
Put bounties on their heads and hunted them like beasts.
This land that was once full of saints and scholars,
Was now taxed to the hilt for pounds and for dollars.
The great famine then came in Eighteen Forty-Five.
The potatoes now rotted in the ground and would not thrive.
Two million died of starvation on the side of the road,
While the English landlords took the food away by the load.
The House of Commons tried earnestly to stop all the dying,
But the Queen said, "Let them die where they are lying."
Two million more were shipped out in rotten sailing ships.
They were used as ballast and thousands died on these trips.
The Queen gave our land away for service and pay,
And she threw out the Irish people and left them for prey.
They slaughtered the rebels and also the fenian men,
And laughed as they killed them without even an amen.
The trail of blood grew deeper as the years went by,
Until the English people could not bear it and asked, "Why?"
Then they voted twice in Commons to give Ireland Home Rule,
But the House of Lords voted no, it's the dream of a fool.
The Irish now saw their hopes dashed again and again.
So they formed the IRA and began to fight in the glen.
They fought and they fought, 'til the island ran red,
With the blood of Irish people as they fell down dead.

The battle went on and lasted six long years,
Irish blood flowed freely and so did the tears.
The battle was then over, but only for some men,
For Ireland was now divided by the English again
They would split us in two whether we liked it or not,
And if we did not like it, why then we would be shot.
Now the soldiers of fortune in the north wanted a state,
And they did not want Ireland as part of their fate.
They split our country in two with the help of the crown.
With agreements from England they would not be let down.
And so today we are here, still at each other's throats,
Because the English gave away our land and also our votes.
Now the blood is flowing freely again on Irish soil,
While the English stand by and let the situation boil.
They do not give a hoot and they don't care what happens to us,
While their soldiers walk on our dead and there is no fuss.
The world also stands by and seems to laugh at us,
Leaving Ireland divided and in such a mess.
It's them Catholics and Protestants is what the English say,
As they point their fingers at us and sit and drink their tea.
The IRA are terrorists and in their propaganda say,
"We must surely kill them off," because that is our way.
We ask, "Who created them?" and they ask us, "Why is that?"
They are not able to answer because they are as blind as a bat.
They are blinded by their trail of blood all across the world,
From China to India, and wherever their flag has been unfurled.
The Empire however, is shrinking and they are now afraid,
Now that their power is dissipating, and with it all their trade.
Ireland's freedom stands out as probably their last hurray,
As they send their army into the north, in foray after foray.
They urge on the Protestants who were planted they say.
And the Queen of England sits quietly on their money and their pay.
Fifteen billion is what she has declared and is now on her books.
The wealthiest woman on this earth and she got it on her looks.
She sits there and refuses to pay for her greatest crime,
And our United Stated Government supports them every time.
It's time for the Irish people across the world to wake up,
And let the British and the Planter know who really is the pup.

They have gotten away with the propaganda game for far too long.
It's time to call their bluff and show that we are really strong.
We must stand up and declare now, who we really are.
So rise up Irish people in Ireland and afar.
And if you cannot lift an arm then why not say a prayer.
Let us free our battered people in Ireland and everywhere.
For the time is right and the dye has been cast.
Ireland will shake off the devil and be Free At Last.

9/4/94

Jerusalem

I stood and looked at her from a hill.
She looked so grand and gave me a thrill.
I had come a long way and now I was here,
Looking at Jerusalem's ramparts so strong and so bare.
I looked across Gethsemane, up the hill to the Golden Gate,
I began to reflect on how Jesus entered and how He sealed our fate.
The Golden Gate is now sealed up and the Temple no longer stands,
Where once so many thousands came, and went back home in bands.
It was the center of life then, where they could come and stay,
For it held the Ark of the Covenant and the people came to pray.
And as I watched and wondered, why it had changed so fast,
I looked over to Calvary, and I began to realize at last,
That the Temple of the Lord was there and no longer in the past.
The Gate of Heaven was bought with His life and now the die is cast
I walked through the Valley of Kidron and up to the Golden Gate,
I trod in Jesus's footsteps where He walked and suffered His fate.
My heart was full of sorrow and I really tried to be brave,
I could hear the whips and lashes as they marched Him to His grave.
It was hard for me to understand how we had made such a mess,
And why the Father stood by and let His Son take all that stress.
But if it had not happened, we would walk around and grope,
And there would be no salvation, leaving us without any hope.
God, however, fulfilled His promises as He foretold in Jeremiah.
That Jesus would come and die on the cross and be our Messiah.

9/1/94

Kindness

Kindness is a string attached to the heart and the mind,
And it carries the vibes to be gentle and kind.
It's a softness that is very visible to the eyes,
And it is always available to anyone who tries.
It's not looking down your nose at a man,
But lifting him up to your place, if you can.
It's stepping beyond without being told.
It's taking a person in from the cold.
It's feeling a warmth that is not from a fire,
Expecting no return or songs from the choir.
It's complementing people when there is reason to.
It's telling them how they look out of the blue.
It's not laying it on so thick they can't stand,
But noticing the little things that make them feel grand.
It's caring for a person a little bit more,
And not sending them out into the cold as before.

3/11/94

Learning To Drive

The time has come and she is sixteen years old
She has taken driver's ed and is ready and bold.
"Lets get my permit, so I can drive your car."
And I begin to worry and visit the bar.
Another one has crossed the sound barrier again.
She is hopping and jumping and can't wait to begin.
She takes her eye test and her book test, too.
She passes both well and now a picture so new.
She picks up her permit and her eyes light up.
I can get behind the wheel and not feel like a pup.
The next thing I hear is, "Can you buy me a car fast?"
I tell her there is another step she has to get past.
And then the day comes for her to take her road test.
Drive slowly and carefully and do your very best.
Obey the laws of the road and be as alert as you can.
Listen carefully to the instructions of the inspection man.
I wait as she goes out for her road test.
I say, "Whatever happens now will be for the best".
When she comes back her face is so white and aglow.
"I passed it!" she said, in spite of going too slow.
And now I am worried because she now can go,
On her own in the hail, the rain, and the snow.
Be careful all you people on the road with a car,
And watch out for my daughter, the driving star.

1/16/94

Life as A Boy

When I was a young boy, I was full of life.
Every day was a joy and there was very little strife.
I walked in the woods and I lay on the grass.
I enjoyed the sun and didn't want the day to pass.
I was able to see the glory of God around me in nature,
Participate in it and appreciate every creature.
I had the patience to stop and just smell the flowers,
Watch as the land was tilled and also climb some towers.
Helped feed the ducks and the chickens and collected the eggs
And gave a hand to my mother as she hung clothes with pegs.
Heard the cuckoo's sound echo in the woods far away,
And listened to the corncrake in the meadow at play.
Waking up in the morning to a "cock-a-doodle-do,"
And thank God there is a full day in front of you.
There was so much to do and life was full of joy,
And that is why it was so wonderful just being a boy.

2/10/94

Loneliness

Loneliness wells up from my flesh and my bone.
It's emptiness and longing to be someplace like home.
It's darkness and sickness that only seems to increase,
It's starvation of the heart and a longing for peace.
It's being ignored and left alone as if unknown.
It's not being loved or touched by my very own.
It's talking to myself and saying I'm a fool.
It's hurting inside for being used as a tool.
It's the dampness and coldness of ice on a tree.
It's the shadow of darkness creeping inside me.
It's having nobody to talk to or listen to my heart.
The touch of a hand is like the warmth of the hearth.
There are so many people walking around in the dark,
With minds and hearts bursting with the loneliness mark,
As they live in a crowded world of selfish decay,
And they never have time to kneel down and pray.
God frees the lonely person and makes them feel loved.
It's a gift of the Holy Spirit from the Heavens above.
Ask and you shall receive, is all you have to do,
And loneliness will vanish because Jesus loves you.

8/26/94

Marriage

Marriage is for grown-ups; that's what they say.
You've got to trust in God and always pray.
There is so much trying to pull us apart,
To devour our love and break our hearts.
The devil hates to see us as a family,
Because the love we have is for eternity.
The children, when born, are such a blessing.
Then as the years go by, we wonder what's missing.
We never seem to talk or hold hands anymore,
No kisses or hugs while saying good-bye at the door.
She used to cook breakfast with a kiss and a smile,
But that day is gone forever for a very long while.
And I wonder whatever happened to love in the sack,
Because all I ever see now is the flat of her back.
And when I ask her gently, what is the matter with her,
"Oh nothing," says she, as if I touched a burr.
Come on now, my love, and open your heart up to me.
I'm your husband of many years, and I long for thee.
Don't let little things stand between us in this way,
And that's because I'm not able to take it day after day.
Let's fight and be clean, and not hit below the belt,
Nor hang it around our necks so it can't be felt.
The world, you know, will always and forever be the same,
For it wants us to go along and play its petty little game.
But, we are a couple and forever we will be,
No matter what the devil tries to do with you and me.
For our love was created in the heavens above,
And no one can shake it, because it's true love.

1/12/94

Memories

I remember well when I was a young boy.
I was free of worries and full of joy.
I took each day and made it full,
Of pleasant places and none were dull.
Our country life was simple and kind.
We played our games and helped the blind.
Our schools were good and very strict.
Our teachers taught us without conflict.
Our food was simple and wholesome with zest.
It came from the farm and was the very best.
We dressed very warm and enjoyed the cold.
We walked or cycled and were seldom bold.
We laughed each day and made up games;
We knew our friends by their first names.
We never felt threatened day or at night,
And only the bogeyman gave us a fright.
We went to our church regularly and loved our God.
And we were always a family with a mom and dad.
They were always there with support and help,
As I started to grow up and become a whelp.
They taught me responsibility and a life that made sense.
And I knew they loved me and there was always recompense.
My parents taught me the basics of honesty and truth,
And now I realize they've stood by me in manhood and youth.

3/3/94

Mother

A mom is always there, you see,
Because that's the way its supposed to be.
She wipes the tears and cleans the cuts.
She kisses the pain good-bye and then puts
The healing touch on all her child's pain,
And seems to do it without any strain.
She watches her kids grow with tender care.
She washes their clothes and combs their hair.
She knows all their worries and feels all their pain.
She teaches them to walk, to talk, and potty train.
They struggle to grow out of their baby skin.
And then they grow up so tall and thin.
Then it's not very long before they are gone away,
Then mother kneels down and begins to pray.
"Lord take care of my child now and every day,
Please help them to be good and not go astray".
Then they fall in love and start their own life.
They become someone else's husband or wife.
But the love of a mother never stops, you see,
Because God created it, and it will always be.

1/8/94

Mother-in-Law

Like mother, like daughter; that is what they say.
I look at my mother-in-law and I begin to pray.
Surely God that's not what is in store for me,
For I've just gotten married to her daughter, you see.
A mother-in-law has always lived up to her reputation,
And she is found every day in the church congregation.
She stirs up the seeds that create anger and love,
and sometimes she is pleasant and as peaceful as a dove.
She dotes on the grandchildren and frowns on the father,
You would think it was her child and not her daughter's.
She comments on everything, and has such an opinion of us.
And when she hurts one of us, she doesn't understand the fuss.
Her face can be read like the Acts of the Apostles.
She makes our home, her home, so she has two castles.
She can do no wrong, and she is good at the tears.
If she is conniving to stay that arouses our fears.
For she doesn't know when she has worn out her stay,
And it's at times like these I begin to pray,
Lord help me to understand my mother-in-law,
So that she doesn't become a bigger pain in the craw.

8/15/94

My Dad

He was tall and slim and we played each day.
He would take us on trips and play in the hay.
He carried us all and swung us around.
He bought us candy and took us to the playground.
And, as time went by we saw his attitude change.
The new house, and the new car were very strange.
He works so hard now, and is gone all the time.
And worries about where he can make the next dime.
I now miss all the good times we had together,
My father, my sister and me, and my younger brother.
Those good times are gone and are no more,
Because, my dad is so busy running out the door.
We're strangers to one another at such a critical time,
When I need him most, and I've started to drink wine.
The man who used to laugh and swing me on the gate,
Is no longer in my life, and now it's too late.
And, when he started to realize I had flown the coop,
I was no longer a child and was out of the loop.
"What happened to the time" is all he could say,
The children are so grown up and no longer want to play.
Father time caught up with all of us, my father and me.
It could have been so much better, just like it used to be.
When life was so much simpler and we were so carefree,
But, money put a stop to that and it wasn't to be.
I watched as he grew older and weaker by the day,
And before I could say I loved him, he passed away.

1/12/94

My Father and My Mother

My father and my mother are old and grey.
They trust in God and always pray.
The years have passed and they are alone.
Their bodies have shrunk and so has their bone.
They are slow getting around and eat very little
They are coughing and choking and throwing up spittle,
They smoke cigarettes like there is no tomorrow,
And if they can't get them, why they just borrow.
Their time is coming and they are prepared,
For a life alone and one they have shared.
So many good times and times they have cried.
They used to be so strong and full of pride.
They were always so vibrant and on the go.
Their eyes so full of sparkle and always aglow.
The years have taken a very great toll.
They are bent, and spent, and no longer bowl.
But there is something about them that sets them apart.
They look like one another and are of the same heart.
Their frailty only brings out the very best,
In their children who always ran to their breasts,
For the roles have changed as if from above,
And now we have a chance to return their love.
We'll love them and keep them as long as we can,
For that is the way it has been since time began.

12/30/93

Pain

Pain makes it's appearance in several ways.
It's fleeting at times and sometimes it stays.
It's the welt from a bat or a kick on the shin.
It's the crack of a fist as it hits my chin.
It's getting sunburned all over while seeking a tan.
It's the spatter of grease from the frying pan.
It's rejection of the girl that I want and I love.
It's something falling on me from high up above.
It's disease and infection, and sometimes a tooth.
It can be physical or mental and sometimes both.
It's losing my job when I need it most.
It's having to tell my wife that hurts the most.
It's watching a loved one as they fade away.
It's the clang of a cell and the price to pay.
It's looking on without being able to help.
It's the starving children or even the whelp.
It's necessary in life and is a warning to us,
That something is wrong and its time to make a fuss.
Life without pain would have no meaning at all.
It would be much like the seasons but missing the fall.
It's a warning device that God built into the body,
Which sometimes only means taking a hot toddy.
It's the birth of a child as its mother screams.
And sometimes the pain is the fulfillment of dreams.
Life without pain is like a car without a battery.
Life cannot begin and there is no flattery.
Now Adam and Eve had it made in the shade,
Then the devil came along and made the good life fade.
Pain then became a part of our life every day,
And only death at the moment can take it away.

8/27/94

Santa Claus

Santa comes at Christmas each year.
The children look for him but never hear
The big man with the large sack of toys
To fill the stockings of the girls and boys.
But Santa won't come and bring a surprise,
Unless they go to bed early and close their eyes.
His reindeer he tethers with leather and bells.
He loads up his sled with toys and then tells,
His reindeer to mush and he is off with a rush,
And the bells begin to jingle and Santa says, "Hush!"
For Santa is gentle, he is forgiving and is kind,
And he hears all the wishes of every child in his mind.
When he reaches the houses, he quietly steals in.
He sees Christmas trees fat, tall, and thin.
He laughs as he reads the requests so bold.
To satisfy all of them he needs a heart of gold.
But, he never fails in his annual chore,
To bring each child's wishes as they sleep and snore.
And when they wake up it's such a surprise,
To see their wishes granted as they rub their eyes.
He came in the night, and I didn't see him.
He drank the milk and ate the cookies in the tin.
I know when I'm older I'm sure I will see,
Santa coming in the sky and laughing with glee.
That never seems to happen, because then I'm told,
You have grown too big and are now too old.
Santa is for the young, the little, and the small,
And now I'm disappointed because I'm too tall.

1/7/94

Sex

Sex was a word that was always said with a hush.
It's something that is done but not in a rush.
We all know it happens and that it is going on.
And we wonder if we are doing it right or wrong.
Some people try to say that it is a dirty word,
But it is one of God's creations just like a bird.
For without it on earth, there would be no people.
It's so natural to us, just like a church steeple.
We should teach it to our children in a loving way,
And maybe then not so many of them would go astray.
It's a gift that awakens in all of us just like Spring,
As we change from our childhood and is a wonderful thing.
Because now we begin to see and experience the joy of life
As we start to grow independent and become husband or wife.
And hopefully we can enjoy sex for the rest of our lives,
For God has ordained it and hopefully our wives.

1/26/94

Snow

I looked out the window and what did I see?
Little white snow flakes falling, one, two, three.
They dance, and they prance, and they weave to and fro.
I try to keep count and wonder where they go.
They disappear into the earth's very core,
And I gaze at the ground and see them no more.
But after a while the snow flakes start to land
And before they disappear they begin to stand.
They build on one another and after a while,
The snow flakes begin to gather and make a big pile.
It is white and soft and covers the street.
A blanket of wool as white as sheep.
It's beauty is deceiving, because it is so cold
And the children love to play in it, joyfully and bold.
They like to build snowmen and throw snowballs,
At each other, as they hide and stoop behind walls.
They laugh and they giggle as they play with the snow.
They get pains in their fingers, and then have to go.
And inside their homes where they are nice and warm,
They stand and look out their windows at the winter storm.
They smile and they think they won't have to go to school.
What a surprise for them now as the sun plays the fool.
The snow melts away and becomes water and then,
It flows into the rivers and is used all over again.

1/4/94

Sounds of the Night

I'm listening now to the sounds of the night.
From dusk to dawn and ending at light.
The scratching of the grasshopper in the thicket.
The croak of the frog and the noise of the cricket.
In the black of night without a hint of light,
The animals play, eat, and talk to our delight.

Tidich, lidich, pidich, and midich,
Fidich, ridich, kidich, and sidich,
Itchi, gitchi, titchi, and pitchi,
Achii, crachii, gachii, and ratchii,
Dadach, gadach, pradach, and madach,
Sadach, badach, tadach, and cadach.

A lilting time of sound without light.
Bringing alive the dark of night.
It's animal life in the trees and grass.
Not known to man who lives behind glass.
A time of safety for the gnats and the bats.
The mice, and the lice, and even the rats.

They hug the trees and hide in the grass.
It's a time of safety from man, alas!
It's their time to eat and have a chat.
A chance to use their radar just like the bat.
To talk to each other and make their sounds,
And at the sign of light return to their mounds.

8/10/94

Spring

I can smell it today in the clear morning air.
It's a freshness that washes over me, so clean and fair.
The spring sun seeps through my body and tells me it's time
That the winter is over and with me that's just fine.
The birds start to whistle, and now I look at the trees,
They are budding and swaying in the gentle spring breeze.
All the animals come alive and are playing about,
Because the earth is awakening and wants to shout,
As new life is seeping through the heart of the earth,
And it is stirring and moving, just like a baby at birth.
The soil that was cold and frozen and dead,
Is now warming and alive, and will bring forth the bread,
To feed the people and animals by the end of the year.
We pray it will be bountiful to eliminate the fear.
The daffodils poke their heads through the soft ground.
The forsythia is yellowing and saying, "I'm around."
The bare trees are sprouting their leaves just like lace,
And are covering all the woods at a very fast pace.
The grass starts to grow and now the earth turns green,
I hear the mowers starting up, and the workers are seen.
The wild geese are heading north in their V so tight,
To nest in the tundra and lay their eggs so white.
The cycle of life is beginning for another year.
The flowers begin to blossom and the bees now appear.
The birds are all back and building nests in the trees.
The squirrels are scampering and scratching at the fleas.
God smiles on the earth and with breath that is blest,
And now life is renewed with such beauty and zest.

2/6/94

The Farmer

The farmer is the man who tills the earth.
It is bred in his body and soul from birth.
He loves the soil and shares in it's growth.
He works day and night, and sometimes both.
He raises up animals and grows grain to feed the earth.
He is subject to the weather and is seldom at the hearth.
He is always on the run, trying to make ends meet.
He is tired and hungry and has mud on his feet.
He prays daily for help from his Almighty God,
As he works hard day and night turning the sod.
He can't sit on his rear or stay in bed after time,
For the animals keep calling to be fed or milking time.
It's a job that starts always at the break of dawn,
And doesn't end in the evening until the sun has gone.
He tills and he sows just as fast as he can.
He reaps and he gathers and sells it to any man.
He milks cows, and feeds pigs until they are fat.
He gathers eggs from the chickens, and sells them at that.
He has tractors to fix and the ploughs that cultivate.
There is no time to waste and it's never too late.
Because the life as a farmer is full of earthly toil,
As he tries to raise his family and prays all the while,
For another good year and a profit would be great,
For all of his hard work and some food on his plate.

2/8/94

Poems of the

Soul

Talk with God

Sit down, sit down, and talk with God.
My life is cluttered, and I feel like a clod.
I've no place to go, and I'm tired and old,
So I come to You, Lord because I'm weary and cold.
I need Your help and graciously ask,
Because only You alone are up to the task.
My mind is scrambled and my heart is down,
My feet are weary and I'm ready to drown.
I'm looking for help and gasping for air.
My soul searches hard, and I wonder if You're there.
I can't touch You, or feel You, but I know You exist.
"Why can't I feel You?" as I slam my fist.
"Lord God, make Your presence known and felt by me,
Come down from Heaven and be a friend I can see."
I reach out to touch You, but there's nobody there,
And I cast my head back, Alas, in despair.
"Lord if I could only talk to You,"
Like son to father and mother, too.
But there the contrast seems the same,
And there is nobody around but myself to blame.
My parents passed away so many years ago today.
I let them die and I am sorry but I forgot to say,
That I loved them very dearly, my mom and dad.
And here I am now growing old and it's also sad,
That I am having the same trouble and I'm without you,
Telling my Lord and My God that, "I love You,"
Why should it be so hard for me to say it that way,
When He died for me on the cross on Good Friday?

12/3/93

Death

The coffin is there in the room, all alone.
The body lies in it and has found a new home.
It's the last place on earth a man wants to be,
But then there is no escaping this fate, you see,
For the time will come for you and for me.
Whether it's early, or late, or after our tea,
We don't want to think about dying or death,
Or giving up everything, even our last breath.
But no matter what we do, father time has us beat.
He will catch up to us at dawn, or in the day's heat,
And we cannot hide or duck this very last meet.
Hopefully we are ready and then it will be a treat.
Now the flowers and the coffin are a nice tradition,
And we hope we go to God and not down to perdition.
So before we die we should place our hope and our trust,
In God's good will long before we turn to dust.

1/13/94

Eyes

The eyes are the window of the soul, they say.
So be careful how you use them night and day.
My father always said to look him straight in the eye,
Because he could tell then if it's the truth or a lie.
It always made me wonder where he came up with that.
Did he read it somewhere or just pull it out of his hat?
I know eyes do not speak but convey so many things,
And they don't have to move or bat like wings.
They are beautiful to behold whether brown, green, or blue,
But watch out for them after they've been drinking the dew.
Now eyes come in all colors and are now changeable, too.
They wink, and the blink, and they say, "I love you."
They are twenty by twenty and then perfect sight.
They are far-sighted, near-sighted, and always a delight.
Without eyes we would trip and fall over everything.
They show us where to go and also the birds on the wing.
What we see every day is just a reflection in our eye,
And this helps us tell if it's the truth or a lie.
Beauty we must realize is only in the eye of the beholder,
And we don't seem to learn this until we are much older.

3/10/94

Forgiveness 1993

I think about what I have done
The good, the bad, and all the fun.
I pray to God to lend an ear,
And forgive my sins for the whole year.
For I am a man full of pride,
I stood by frozen as my wife cried.
She saw through me and prayed I would change,
But all I could do was rearrange
The anger and stupidity that was part of me.
It would take great effort to change, you see.
I reached out to her and said, "Please forgive me."
For I loved her in my heart and soul, you see.
I have offended her many times in my life
And forgotten the vows that I made to my wife.
She was pretty, and beautiful and such a good soul.
The children, work, and worries have taken their toll.
She does her best now to look pretty and wise.
She has gained some weight but still is a prize.
And as I grow older I've learned to appreciate
All the good things about her, and the joys of late.
But sometimes I wonder if I've waited too long
To tell her I love her and it's not a swan song.
May God have mercy and always love me,
For without God I'm nothing and lost in a sea.
My wife and I are a creation of God's love,
Put together by Him in the Heavens above.
And someday we'll join Him, me and my wife,
When He has decided it's the end of our life

1/1/94

God

Our God is in Heaven and on the earth.
He is full of life, like a baby at birth.
He grows on us and loves us just like a child,
Providing we let him and are forgiving and mild.
We must open our eyes and look around and see,
How pleasant life really is and can really be.
He is not complicated and He is full of love.
He gave us His only Son and also the Dove.
And all we have to do is accept Him and live,
A life so calm and serene and learn to give.
So why don't we hand over our lives to our God;
And not be burdened daily with turning the sod.
He feeds all the animals and the birds in the air.
You don't see them dying or living in despair.
All we need is the faith of the small mustard seed.
It's a small thing he asks and not a mighty deed.
Then why not turn over our body and our soul,
To our God and our maker which in the end is our goal.

1/25/94

Hope

Hope springs from the soul of man,
It's invisible, powerful, and part of God's plan.
It sends energy to my mind, my heart, and my soul.
It strengthens my body and makes me feel whole.
It's light, and fire, and food and drink,
And is usually generated by pen and ink.
It makes me smile and beam all over.
It's refreshing and clean like the smell of clover.
It strengthens my legs, my heart, and my mind.
It tempers my soul and makes it kind.
Without hope I would just fade away and die,
And with it all my dreams and my will to try.
Hope is the Spirit of God in my soul,
It's showing me the way and giving me a goal.

8/24/94

Sunday, A Day of Rest

Sunday is always a day of rest.
We get up early and put on our best.
We gather our family around us for tea,
Then go to Church to be with Thee.
Our souls need strengthening on this day,
So we join our people to sing and pray
To the Father, the Son, and the Spirit above,
Seeking help and strength to renew our love.
Then the Holy Spirit quietly descends on us,
And blesses our family without any fuss.
We sing songs of praise and glory to You
We ask for intercession by the saints, too.
And when we are finished we offer ourselves up,
And we join with the priest as he drinks from the cup.
He gives himself to us at the breaking of the bread.
We take and we eat, just as He said.
We are thankful to be in such a free country today,
Where people are allowed to gather and to pray.
We bow our heads down as we kneel in a line,
And thank God again for the bread and wine.
Without You, Lord, there is no meaning to life,
Just seven days of work of push and strife.
So, thank You again for this day of rest,
May we enjoy it in peace with love and zest.

1/8/94

The Bread of Life

Two thousand years ago in a room in Jerusalem,
The last supper took place and they said, "Amen."
Jesus raised up the bread and the cup to the sky,
And said, "Eat and drink for soon I will die.
In memory of me I give you this feast,
To save all of you and conquer the beast.
Forever I give you My flesh and My blood,
And promise you again there will be no flood."

A new life then started and forever will last,
And He promised His second coming would be a real blast.
The heavens will open and the sky will clear,
And the Son of Man and His mother will appear.
The Angels and Ancients will all gather around,
And cry "Holy, Holy" as they kneel on the ground.
The earth will awaken with love and with joy.
To celebrate Jesus with songs and a great cry.

Jesus gave His life up to save all mankind.
A sacrifice like this just boggles the mind.
We mocked Him and whipped Him, and crowned Him with thorns.
We spat on Him, jeered Him, and even blew horns.
We led Him to the slaughter, amid cries and jeers.
We hung Him on a cross and we drank some beers.
We watched as he died in terrible pain,
And His blood washed away the sin and the stain.

Jesus looked up to Heaven and before He did die,
Said, "Father forgive them," which was His last cry.
So now we have the Bread of Life to save us from sin,
To help us live a better life and strengthen us within.
Mass is celebrated by His people every hour and every day,
As we eat His body and drink His blood in the very same way.
And today we thank the Father for the Holy Spirit and His Son,
For They give our life meaning and helps us become one.

12/5/93

The Church

It sits on a hill in the middle of our town.
It's tall with a steeple that looks like a crown.
It's God's home, they say, and in it He's found,
And we go there on Sunday and give Him a pound.
While all the people around are praying and singing,
And the boys in the tower keep the chapel bells ringing,
As they pull on the ropes that are long and strong,
And enjoy every minute of it, as the bells go bing-bong.
The preacher stands up in the pulpit and prays,
For everyone in the church and those in their graves.
And the people join in as the choir begins to sing.
That song is so familiar and has such a good ring.
God, give us our daily bread and take care of the crops.
Give us food for our tables and plenty for the shops.
Take care of our kids and help them on their way,
To grow up in a free country and always to pray.
For my church, my Lord, is a place of hope and love,
And that's why we gather together to praise you above.
For our trust is in You, and it is easy to see,
Why our country is so prosperous and has always been free.
So help us, Lord, not to forget how You blessed us,
With the gifts of love and peace that are so precious.

1/25/94

The Crucifixion

They took Him from the garden of Gethsemane.
He went like a lamb, and they mocked Him with glee.
They had a purpose in mind from the very beginning,
With treachery in their hearts, they knew they were sinning.
They took Jesus to Caiaphas and to Pilate, too.
They trumped up charges that would turn the air blue.
"This Man has done no wrong," is all the Roman could say,
And "so I give you Barrabas and Jesus today."
The crowd shouted out and said "Take Him away,
Give us Barrabas and let Jesus stay."
Thirty pieces of silver and a traitorous kiss,
And the crowd shouted out, "Crucify Him," with a hiss.
They led Him off and stripped Him down.
They flailed his back and put on a crown.
They put on a robe and then led Him away to be crucified,
While His disciples and His mother stood there and cried.
They saddled Him with a very large cross.
They whipped Him and Mocked Him saying, "Now who's the boss?"
He fell and He bled and was racked with pain,
As He climbed up this rock with such a terrible strain.
And when they got there, they stripped off his cloak,
They mocked Him and hit Him and began to joke,
"Hail King of the Jews," as they hit Him on the head,
The crown of thorns sunk in, and he freely bled.
They threw Him on the ground and stretched out His hands,
They nailed them to the cross and His feet to the stand.
His groans and His moans could be heard a long way,
And His friends and apostles ran away in dismay.
The Romans raised the cross up for everyone to see,
"Hail King of the Jews," they shouted with glee.
He hung there and died in such terrible pain,
While His blood was shed and He cleansed our stain.
The whole world trembled and the Sanctuary was rent in two,
But He said, "Father, forgive them for they know not what they do."
Then He died on the cross, and our sins were forgiven,
And now we were able to enter into Heaven.

3/12/94

The Priest

I see him dressed in his long black robes.
Dedicated to God and full of high hopes.
His home is where his people are.
His bed is hard and his cupboard is bare.
Go feed my lambs and feed my sheep.
Don't worry about where you will eat or sleep.
He must be strong and have great faith,
To make this commitment and seal his fate.
To trust in God and place his life,
In Gods hands like a man and wife.
It's a love that spans an eternity,
Like the Father, and the Son in the Trinity.
It's the Spirit of joy, and love, and grace,
That is reflected only from God's face.
He's a direct descendent from Peter and Paul.
Continuing in time and never will fall.
Given his power by our God Divine.
Changing into His body, using bread and wine.
How precious a gift our priests are to us.
How we take them for granted without any fuss.
May God always provide us with a good priest,
Who will help us daily to conquer the beast.
We pray for him each day and in God we trust,
And thank you for the blessing bestowed on us.

8/23/94

Resurrection

They took Him from the cross before His body was cold,
And while lying dead in the arms of His mother's fold.
She looked at His body and was very upset
To see what they had done to her little pet.
His body had been torn and beaten to death.
She hugged Him and kissed Him until He was all wet.
She washed and she cleaned Him and combed His hair
She was careful, gentle, and full of care.
She wrapped Him in a cloak of soft, white linen,
And the Sabbath was close and no tomb to lay Him in.
So, Joseph of Arimathaea came forth and offered his own
To lay her Son down before they went home.
They closed up the tomb with a very large stone,
And they went to their homes with a cry and a moan.
The Sanhedrin sent soldiers to guard the stone
They didn't trust His disciples to leave him alone.
On the third day the stone was thrust away,
And Jesus came forth in all His glorious array.
The splendor of the light took the soldiers by surprise,
And they ran away frightened as they saw Jesus rise.
He came forth in splendor like the light of the sun,
And the Angels cried, "Hosanna!" and paid homage to the Son.
For Jesus had conquered all sin by His death,
And the Apostles stood around and began to fret.
He appeared to them daily and they knew He was not dead,
And recognized Him each time by the breaking of the bread.

1/1/94

The Second Coming

He told us very clearly that He would come again.
It would be His second coming and we all said "Amen."
Nobody knows when it's going to be, night or day.
So I think I better kneel down and begin pray.
He is going to come like a thief in the night.
And those who are ready will get a great fright.
He will separate the good from the bad on that day,
And all who have not repented will surely pay.
For the warnings have been clear and very plain,
And those who are caught will cry with disdain.
Then the Lord will appear with splendor and might,
and all who see Him will wonder at the sight.
The Angels on high will blow their trumpets like mad,
And separate the world into the good and the bad.
The serpent will be cast down into a fiery hell,
And all those who followed him will join him and yell.
For they have been vanquished there until the end of time,
And the remainder will join Jesus in the sublime,
To live forever and share the heavens above,
And be always surrounded by joy and love.

1/6/94

The Spirit of God

Into the flesh of man He seeps,
To awaken his soul, and now he weeps.
For the breath of God is so refreshing,
It's the essence of life and also a blessing.
I grasp for things daily and only find air,
Even though I know God's Grace is beyond compare.

Man started out on the right side.
He ate the apple and then tried to hide.
Then Jesus came and gave us a way out.
And the Angels in Heaven taught us to shout.
Come Holy Spirit and in my heart and soul,
Take your rightful place and make me whole.

I'm lost without the light of God.
Come Holy Spirit like a lightning rod.
Enlighten my mind and brighten my soul.
Refresh my body and make it whole.
I stand in awe at Your Majesty and Might,
As I bow my head in prayer this very night.

You are my God, and You alone.
Sit high above everyone on Your Throne.
You are so merciful and You saw our plight,
You sent Your only Son, and what a delight.
You saved us from death, and the pain of hell.
You gave us Your Spirit within us to dwell.

You are my Hero, and I depend on You.
My weaknesses are many and my sins are, too.
I ask Your forgiveness and long to be whole,
By allowing Your Spirit to enter my soul.
You have forgiven me ten times ten, and more,
For You are my God that I love and adore.

Awaken mankind to the flesh of God,
As the Son of Man on the earth He trod.
His miracles were seen and His word made flesh.
For all of us to see and so we could start afresh.
The fire of God can now enter our heart,
And we can be one with Him if we are smart.

His promises are great and simple and true.
Ask anything in His name and He will give you,
A reservation in Heaven and a life of joy.
No need for money, there's nothing to buy.
For God is goodness, happiness, and love.
He removes all weakness when we join Him above.

8/12/94

Temptation

Temptation is the enticement to make me waiver,
From the God given gifts of our Lord and Saviour.
It's the pleading and cajoling to cross over the line,
With promises of wonders that are alluring and sublime.
It's playing with my feelings to want some more,
Of sex and possessions and promises galore.
It's dangling before me all my desires and my needs.
It's planting his evil and all the devils bad seeds.
It's presenting all the lures of the devil and his kind,
And challenging my body, and soul, and my mind.
It's conjuring up visions of grandeur and might,
That appear so beautiful, especially to my sight.
It's the allure of something that is my heart's desire,
And when I accept it, it usually turns into a quagmire.
It's the diamond that glows to make me go astray,
As I try to walk the right path day after day.
It's only with God's help that I am willing and able,
To overcome temptation and keep my life stable.

8/28/94

What Does It Profit a Man?

Man can spend his time working and tilling the soil.
He can also change his mind and go looking for oil.
Or better still, he may be more adventurous and bold.
He could go into the mountains looking for gold.
The grass is always green on the other side of the hill.
Man never seems to stop and think of the bill,
for the price can be greater than what we think.
We may loose our soul and not even blink.
The joy of living is not in the sky,
But under our feet and in every try.
For the Lord has stated it, year after year,
And He sent His only Son down at a price so dear,
To save all mankind from sin and fear.
He loved us so much and He made it very clear,
That there is something else better than money and beer.
So, come along and pray and sing out loud without fear,
What does it profit a Man, when the price is so great.
To loose your soul eternally and have to pay the freight.
Lord, thank you for giving us hope and good cheer,
Every day of the week and throughout the year.

1/7/94

Wisdom

Wisdom is a book in the Old Testament.
It's full of knowledge and tells us to repent.
It's the ability to see what is good in the world,
And not being bothered by the milk being curdled.
It's knowing the difference between right and wrong,
While listening to people, the weak and the strong.
It's knowing that knowledge is a very large tree,
That is designed especially for you and for me.
The key to all wisdom is knowing who it's from.
It's built into a family and especially the mom.
For wisdom is a special gift granted by God,
And He gave it to His followers wherever they trod.
It is judgement, and mercy and a very full life.
It helps people out when there is strife,
For it is God in His goodness holding out His hand,
To His favorite human being living on this land.

3/8/94